MW00578678

EDITED BY DEBRA KELLER

ILLUSTRATED BY LISA PARETT

ARIEL BOOKS

**Andrews McMeel
Publishing**

Kansas City

Illustrations copyright © 2002 by Lisa Parett

ISBN: 0-7407-2752-4
Library of Congress Catalog Card Number:
2002102330

iNTRODUCTiON

If you're like most people, the older you get, the less you look forward to BiRTHDAYS. You start out counting years and end up counting candles (or

7

maybe the lines in your face). Whoa! STOP! Being your age can't be *all* bad. After all, think back to when you were younger. Remember all the things you couldn't *wait* to leave behind: teenage acne, first job jitters, relationship troubles, credit cards out of control, the early years of running your own business. Aren't you glad some of that is over?

Plenty of people LOVE the age they've attained, whether it's twenty-five, fifty, or eighty. They enjoy increased

HAPPY BIRTHDAY!

MATURITY, a feeling of accomplishment, and the wisdom of real experience. And this doesn't mean they've stopped the party; they just don't let the party get the best of them!

Read on to gather some AGELESS birthday wit and wisdom. See how the rich and famous and the not so rich and famous celebrate each personal anniversary. Think of the passing years not as a speeding conveyor belt but as the finest virtual reality tour ever invented. MANY HAPPY RETURNS!

I do like being how

OLD I am.

I'm so glad the vicissi-

tudes . . . have subsided.

—*Meg Ryan*

HAPPY BIRTHDAY!

I try to ignore

AGING

because there's nothing

I can do.

—*Sally Field*

BIRTHDAY WIT

You can deny your age, even deny your birth-day, but you can't deny you were born.

HAPPY BIRTHDAY!

BIRTHDAY WISDOM

If you don't like surprises,
never, ever answer the door
wearing old pajamas, fuzzy
slippers, hair curlers, or a
mud mask anywhere near
your birthday.

13

CELEBRITY BIRTHDAYS

Miss Piggy	May 25
Bugs Bunny	July 27
Mickey Mouse	November 18

HAPPY BIRTHDAY!

In 1972, I eliminated all
years from my life. I don't
keep track of anything by
years or weeks. I call it my
living experiment.

—*Jack Nicholson*

15

MY BEST BIRTHDAY EVER WAS . . .

HAPPY BIRTHDAY!

my FORTY-FIRST.

To make up for forgetting my fortieth my husband planned a week of surprises including a San Francisco Bay cruise, a play, two dinners, a ballet, a movie, and a party with family and friends.

—*Elaine, Sacramento, CA*

17

ONCE upon a time, there was a girl who led a life filled with beautiful friends and wonderful mistakes, and one day she woke up and realized that and began to live infinitely HAPPILY ever since.

—*Julia Roberts*

AGE is

nothing more than
experience, and
some of us are
more experienced
than others.

— *Mickey Rooney*

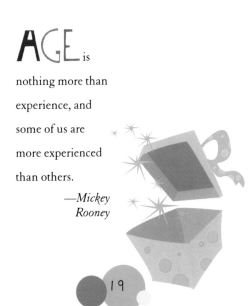

19

DRESS-UP, ANYONE?

John Stamos, former star of the TV series *Full House,* isn't one to celebrate quietly. For his THIRTY-SIXTH BIRTHDAY he and his wife Rebecca Romijn-Stamos threw a cross-dressing party. "Rebecca came as me in the '80s, with a really bad wig," said Stamos.

HAPPY BIRTHDAY!

He dressed up as his supermodel wife, but he wore two different outfits during the evening. He started out as a FRENCH MAID, then changed into "a patent leather skirt and a feather boa. I think I was the ugliest woman I've ever seen."

21

BIRTHDAY
WIT

If you're worried about
what the years are doing
to your figure, don't look
behind you.

HAPPY BIRTHDAY!

BIRTHDAY
WISDOM

Your birthday lets the
people who love you love
you a little bit more.

23

At FORTY-THREE,
I've never felt better in my
life. Much more grounded
and very sexy. I feel like a
juicy piece of fruit.

—*Sela Ward*

HAPPY BIRTHDAY!

I'm about to be FORTY,
and I'm still sort of a
younger leading man . . .
not in life, but in movies,
in the world of leading
men.

—*George Clooney*

25

MY BEST BIRTHDAY EVER WAS . . .

HAPPY BIRTHDAY!

the year I turned SEVEN.
We were living in northern India, in a small town with no electricity. My father rented an elephant for me and my friends to ride, and a Ferris wheel that had to be cranked by hand.
—*Harold, Arcata, CA*

Nobody understands
anyone EIGHTEEN,
including those who are
eighteen.

—*Jim Bishop*

CELEBRITY BIRTHDAYS

Kermit the Frog	September 24
Homer Simpson	May 10
Marge Simpson	refuses to divulge

I'm the kind of person who looks at

what I'm doing NOW.

I don't like to look back.

—*Nadia Comaneci*

31

SIXTY-ONE FOR SIXTY-ONE

MARK MCGWIRE might not have been

thinking "birthday gift" when he ripped

his sixty-first homer of the 1998 season,

but his timing (both on and off the field)

couldn't have been better. His father, John,

was celebrating his sixty-first birthday at

HAPPY BIRTHDAY!

the time. But the elder McGwire wasn't surprised by the coincidence: "He told me that he was going to hit sixty-one for my birthday. He's a man of his word."

BIRTHDAY
WIT

All birthdays are great
if you consider the
alternative.

HAPPY BIRTHDAY!

BIRTHDAY WISDOM

The key to aging gracefully is learning the art of acceptance.

35

It's great getting

OLD.

—*Harrison Ford*

HAPPY BIRTHDAY!

Hair and **TEETH.**

If a man got those two things,

he got it all.

—*James Brown*

37

MY BEST BIRTHDAY EVER WAS...

HAPPY BIRTHDAY!

not on my birthday. **SIX MONTHS** away from my birthday some friends and I went out to dinner. At the end of the meal all the waiters and waitresses gathered around us and sang Happy Birthday to someone. I sang too, until a waitress placed a piece of cake in front of *me!*

—Liz, *Pleasant Hill, CA*

When I was a kid, I didn't really think about turning FORTY. But now I'm digging coming into it. I am in the best physical shape I have ever been, and I have the benefit of some wisdom that comes with having lived.

—*Melissa Etheridge*

HAPPY BIRTHDAY!

Languor is underrated. Bone-lazy idle-
ness, hours spent staring at the sky and
remembering books and BIRTHDAYS
and great kisses: This is a pure pleasure
that eludes the productive in all their
confident superiority. Languor is sunny
and hot.

—*Kevin Patterson*

41

BIRTHDAY WIT

The secret of eternal youth is to learn how to lie well.

HAPPY BIRTHDAY!

BIRTHDAY WISDOM

Your birthday is a celebration of you. Why not give yourself the best present ever?

43

LAVERNE AND LEIA

Actor and writer **CARRIE FISHER**, who

got her start as Princess Leia in *Star Wars,*

and director **PENNY MARSHALL**, first

famous as Laverne in the TV series

Laverne and Shirley, both celebrate a birth-

day in October. Close friends for nearly

two decades, they try to throw a joint party

every year. "We invite everybody," says

Marshall. They don't like to miss the date:

When Fisher's marriage to PAUL SIMON

got in the way one year, Marshall tagged

along on the honeymoon!

45

When it's a good time, I CELEBRATE. When it's a bad time, I also celebrate. Know what I mean?

—*Goldie Hawn*

MY BEST BIRTHDAY EVER WAS....

HAPPY BIRTHDAY!

THIRTY-FOURTH. I won

the first duathlon I had ever entered, qualified for the world record, defended my dissertation and passed, officially got my title as "Dr." and Ph.D., turned thirty-four, and was thrown a party by my closest friends—all in two days.

—*Sarah, Cambridge, MA*

CELEBRITY BIRTHDAYS

Pebbles Flintstone	February 22
Donald Duck	June 6
Daffy Duck	April 17

HAPPY BIRTHDAY!

You supposedly
get DIFFERENT as
you get older. I'm
not so aggressive.
I'm not so ready to
punch people out
as I used to be.

—*Mick Jagger*

51

I want to keep my own defini-
tion of MYSELF. I just want
to keep growing up a little bit—
and growing out.

—*Meg Ryan, on getting older*

BIRTHDAY WIT

You're only as old as you admit.

HAPPY BIRTHDAY!

BIRTHDAY
WISDOM

The longer you've lived, the more you've loved.

55

When you are ETGHTEEN, you
are not obsessed by youth. After thirty,
you have to make an effort to look young.
This is the drama of life.

—*Karl Lagerfeld*

HAPPY BIRTHDAY!

I'm getting toward MIDDLE AGE, and I've set my goals. I might make it, might not. But I will look back to say I tried.

—*Carl Lewis*

57

A TOAST TO BRANDY

Actor and singer BRANDY celebrated her eighteenth birthday in style . . . and en masse, surrounded by nearly five hundred party guests, including classmates from Pepperdine University, costars from her weekly series *Moesha,* pro basketball

HAPPY BIRTHDAY!

player Kobe Bryant, and her parents.

"All my favorite stars, my family, and my friends are here," said Brandy. "I'm having the happiest birthday that an eighteen-year-old girl could ever have."

MY BEST BIRTHDAY EVER WAS...

HAPPY BIRTHDAY!

FIFTEENTH.

My friend (and secret love) Neil had been working as an intern at the Metropolitan Museum of Art in the costume collection. The night before my birthday, they were having a very hoity-toity gala opening, to which Neil invited me. I met Cher, Mick and Bianca Jagger, and Diana Vreeland. Sometime during the train ride home midnight struck and I turned fifteen.

—*Karen, Bethel, CT*

I absolutely refuse to

reveal my

AGE.

What am I? A car?

—*Cyndi Lauper*

HAPPY BIRTHDAY!

I felt like my clothes finally

FIT

and I didn't have to

be anything other than myself.

—*Meryl Streep,*
on reaching middle age

63

BIRTHDAY WIT

You're only as old as
you feel . . . if you
avoid looking in
mirrors.

HAPPY BIRTHDAY!

BIRTHDAY WISDOM

One good thing about growing old is that you can speak your mind and get away with it.

65

CELEBRITY BIRTHDAYS

Snoopy	October 2
Garfield	June 19
Wile E. Coyote	September 17

HAPPY BIRTHDAY!

Certain aspects of my
youth are over. I still
like to have a rockin'
good time, but I don't
like to inflict perma-
nent damage.

—*Woody Harrelson*

67

I think there were a lot of years in my life when I wasn't so happy, because I was CONFUSED, [but] as long as you grow and come out the other side of it, then it's all worth it.

—*Drew Barrymore*

HAPPY BIRTHDAY!

I am having a GOOD TIME, but people who say they are happy turning forty are lying. I would give up the wisdom of forty to be twenty-two again.

—*Scott Baio*

69

MY BEST BIRTHDAY EVER WAS . . .

HAPPY BIRTHDAY!

my TWENTY-NINTH. My husband turned the whole thing into a joke by throwing me a surprise thirtieth birthday party. Nothing was as it seemed. Waitresses rummaged through our purses to find lipstick they liked, waiters took our orders but brought us all the same thing, clean ashtrays were replaced with dirty ones—it went on like this all night.

—Debbie, Palo Alto, CA

71

Turning

FORTY?

I really don't pay attention

to it.

—*Dennis Rodman*

I look in the

MIRROR

and I like what I see.

—*Nadia Comaneci,*
on growing older

73

ROYAL WIT AND WISDOM

On the morning of her ninetieth birthday, Britain's "QUEEN MUM," mother of Elizabeth II, took an unexpected stroll among the waiting crowd of well-wishers. To a fan who made her a gift of premixed gin and tonic, she replied, "I'll drink that

HAPPY BIRTHDAY!

later." When a seven-year-old boy asked

if he could be king, she told him, "You'll

have to work very hard." Good advice,

indeed, to anyone with ambitions, royal

or otherwise.

One of the great things about being FIFTY . . . is the absolute concrete assurance that women my age will never be considered for one of these macho, airhead, testosterone action films.

—*Jessica Lange*

HAPPY BIRTHDAY!

I have this growing
sense of morality, this
feeling that everything
I do is recorded. . . .
My SPIRITUAL

questioning is at
an all-time high.

—*Carly Simon, on
getting older*

When I was **24,44** seemed like **104!** But my strengths now come from experience. I feel like I've come into my own.

—*Sally Field*

HAPPY BIRTHDAY!

I'll live

FOREVER,

but I may not be able to move.

—Katharine Hepburn,
at eighty-three

79

Set in Elegant

Garamond and

Hatmaker

at SNAPHAUS
GRAPHICS in

Dumont, NJ